D0548065

THE One & Only tapas and appetisers Cookbook

NEW HOLLAND

THE One & Only tapas and appetisers Cookbook

All the recipes you will ever need

With a Foreword by
Jenny Linford

NEW
HOLLAND

First published by New Holland Publishers in 2012
London • Cape Town • Sydney • Auckland

www.newhollandpubishers.com

86 Edgware Road, London W2 2EA, United Kingdom

Wembley Square, Solan Road, Gardens, Cape Town 8001, South Africa

1/66 Gibbes Street, Chatswood, NSW 2067, Australia
www.newholland.com.au

218 Lake Road, Northcote, Auckland 0746, New Zealand

Created by
Pulp Media, Richmond, London

Project Editors: Emma Wildsmith and Helena Caldon
Art Director: Susi Martin
Illustrations: Kuo Kang Chen

Photography: Charlotte Tolhurst, Stockfood Ltd, Philip Wilkins: 60-61, 84-85, 128-129, 172-173, 194-195, Shutterstock.com: 1, 2, 6, 10, 14, 17, 18, 223, 224-5, 232-233, 238-239.
Every effort has been made to credit photographers and copyright-holders. If any have been overlooked we will be pleased to make the necessary corrections in subsequent editions.

Publisher: James Tavendale
www.pulp.me.uk

A record of this book is available from the National Library.
ISBN 9781742572475
Printed in Italy
10 9 8 7 6 5 4 3 2 1

"Appetizers are the little
things you keep eating until you
lose your appetite."

Joe Moore

Contents

Foreword

By Jenny Linford

There is a definite charm to being served an assorted medley of small platefuls of tasty food to graze upon. No wonder, then, that so many cuisines feature versions of these appealing dishes, from Lebanese mezze to the Danish smorgasbord. In Spain, tapas are traditionally served in bars as an accompaniment to alcoholic drinks such as sherry, cava or wine. The word 'tapas' means 'lid' or 'cover' and its gastronomic use is thought to have originated in the custom of covering a glass of wine with a complimentary little plate of something to nibble on. Small plates are gloriously versatile, since they can be served as canapés at parties, as a first course or used in combination to make up an entire 'grazing' meal.

Entertaining tips

If you're planning to cook an assortment of tapas or small plates for a meal or a party, then bear the following advice in mind.

Pace yourself

When choosing which dishes to cook, don't be overly ambitious. Avoid choosing dishes that all need to be made at the last minute; make sure that some can be made in advance. Similarly, opt for a mixture of simple and more elaborate recipes. As the host, you want to be relaxed and welcoming, not harassed and stressed.

Offer a range

The great thing about serving a medley of little dishes is that you can offer something to suit everyone's taste. When it comes to deciding on dishes, make sure that your selection is varied, ranging across fish and seafood, meat and vegetables. Use a variety of cooking techniques, from steaming to grilling or shallow-frying. You're looking to serve a selection of dishes which both complement and contrast with each other: hot and cold, raw and cooked, mild and spicy.

Ensure eye appeal

Presentation is very important. Choose a colourful selection of dishes and garnish them appealingly with, for example, chopped fresh green herbs such as parsley, mint or chives, a delicate sprinkling of red paprika or a few garnet-like fresh pomegranate seeds.

Pace the meal

While generosity is always appealing, do remember that appetisers really should be appetisers; stimulants to the appetite before the main course rather than seriously substantial.

Go for the best

When cooking simple recipes where the quality of the ingredients used can make or break the dish, do make sure you find the best and freshest foodstuffs where possible, especially when it comes to seafood, fish or salad vegetables.

How to deep-fry successfully

Of the many diverse cooking techniques used in creating small dishes, one of the most popular is deep-frying, used to add an appetising crispness to dishes from whitebait to arancini (little balls of rice). When it comes to deep-frying at home, an automatic deep fat fryer is very simple to use, but not at all essential. For the best results follow these rules:

• Use good-quality oil with a high smoking point, such as groundnut oil or maize oil.

• Use a deep-sided pan such as a wok or a deep-fat fryer and be generous with your cooking oil. As the term implies, 'deep-frying' means completely immersing the ingredients in hot oil so that they cook evenly and thoroughly.

• Heat your oil to the right temperature before you add in any ingredients. If it's not hot enough they'll absorb the oil and be unappealingly greasy; if the oil is too hot, though, the outside of the food will burn before the centre is cooked through. Most deep-frying takes place at between 300-350 degrees Fahrenheit/150-175 degrees Centigrade. The simplest way to check that the oil has reached the required temperature is to use a deep fry or candy thermometer. Alternately, test the temperature by placing a cube of bread in the hot oil. If it turns golden-brown in around 40 seconds, then your oil is ready for deep-frying.

• Don't over-crowd your pan. Adding ingredients into the hot oil lowers its temperature, so take care not to add in too much at once otherwise the deep-frying process slows down, resulting in greasy food.

• **Never** leave oil that is heating unattended. Oil is highly flammable, so it's very important to keep an eagle eye on it and be vigilant at all times while deep-frying.

• As soon as your ingredients are cooked through, remove them with a slotted spoon and drain at once on kitchen paper to remove any excess oil before serving.

Aubergine rolls stuffed with goats' cheese and spinach

1. Preheat the oven to 350°F (180°C).

2. Cut the aubergine into thin slices lengthways and sprinkle with salt to draw out any bitter juice to come out. After 30 minutes, dab off any liquid that may have seeped out, and brush the slices with olive oil.

3. Mix the ricotta with the goats' cheese, breadcrumbs, pine nuts, sultanas and wilted spinach.

4. Heat up a griddle pan to high temperature and cook the aubergine slices until griddle marked on both sides.

5. Take a slice of aubergine and place a tbsp of the cheese mixture at one end. Roll the aubergine slices and place in a baking dish. Continue with the rest of the aubergine slices and cheese.

6. Bake in the oven for 15 mins before removing and serving.

Preparation time: 30 min
Cooking time: 15 min
Serves 10

Ingredients:
1 Aubergine
100g Ricotta
125gsoft goats' cheese
4 tbsp breadcrumbs
1 tbsp golden sultanas
2 tbps toasted pine nuts
100g wilted spinach
1 tbsp extra virgin olive oil
Salt and pepper, to taste

Marinated fish salad

1. Add half of the lemon and lime juice to the fish and scallops, mix well and place in the fridge for 2 hours to marinate. After marinating, drain and discard the juice.

2. Add the fish to a ziplock bag along with the remaining lemon and lime, oregano, sherry vinegar, onion, cumin, olive oil and pepper. Place in the fridge for 8 hours or overnight.

3. Chop the skinned tomato and add to the fish mixture.

4. Sprinkle with the chopped flat leaf parsley to serve.

Preparation time: 15 min
   plus overnight marinating
Serves 1 portion tapas

150ml lemon juice
150ml lime juice
150g fresh salmon, cut into cubes
4 fresh scallops, thinly sliced
1 tbsp chopped fresh oregano
1 tsp sherry vinegar
1 small red onion
¼ tsp ground cumin
1 tbsp Spanish olive oil
¼ tsp white pepper
1 medium-sized tomato, peeled and
   deseeded
1 tbsp chopped flat leaf parsley

Spicy meatballs with tomato sauce

Preparation time: 15 min
Cooking time: 25 min
Serves 15

For the meatballs:
50g soft chorizo
250g minced beef
2 garlic cloves, finely chopped
1 small onion, finely chopped
2 tbsp breadcrumbs
3 tbsp flat leaf parsley, roughly
  chopped
salt and pepper, to taste
100g plain flour

For the tomato sauce:
1 small onion, finely chopped
1 tsp sweet paprika
2 garlic cloves, finely chopped
olive oil
splash of red or white wine
300g passata
1 tsp dried thyme
1 bay leaf

1. Add the chorizo and mince to a food processor and pulse until combined. Put the mince mixture in a bowl along with the garlic, onion, breadcrumbs, flat leaf parsley, and season with salt and pepper. Mix together and form walnut-sized balls, roll in flour, and leave to one side whilst you prepare the tomato sauce.

2. To make the tomato sauce, gently fry the onion, paprika and garlic in a little olive oil until transparent. Turn up the heat before adding in a good splash of wine and cook for 30 seconds. Turn the heat to a low setting and add in the passata, thyme and bay leaf, and cook for a further 10 minutes.

3. Heat a little oil in a non-stick frying pan and add in the meatballs. Cook for about 10 minutes or until brown all over and no longer pink inside.

4. To serve, spoon the sauce into the base of a tapas dish and sit the meatballs on top.

Pepper salad with sherry vinegar, garlic and oil

1. Place the peppers under a hot grill, turning them often until the skins have turned black and charred all over. Remove from the grill, peel the skin and remove the stalks and seeds.

2. Slice the peppers into strips and place in a bowl.

3. Mix the sherry vinegar with the garlic and olive oil. Pour this mixture over the pepper and stir to combine.

4. Sprinkle with the flat leaf parsley and serve.

Preparation time: 5 min
Cooking time: 25 min
Serves 1 portion of tapas

2 green pepper
2 red peppers
10ml sherry vinegar
1 garlic clove
20ml extra virgin olive oil
2 tbsp flat leaf parsley

Mini fish frikadellas

1. Soak the bread in the warm milk.

2. Heat 2 tablespoons oil in a frying pan and fry the shallots until soft.

3. Squeeze out the excess liquid from the bread and put into a bowl with the shallots, fish, eggs, herbs, salt and pepper, and mash to a purée. If the mixture is too soft, add some breadcrumbs. Shape the mixture into bite-sized patties.

4. Heat the remaining oil and fry the patties in batches, for about 3–4 minutes on each side, until golden brown. Serve on cocktail sticks.

Preparation time: 15 min
Cooking time: 15 min
Serves 15–20

100g sliced bread
250ml warm milk
5 tbsp oil
2 shallots, chopped
800g cod fillet, finely chopped
3 eggs, beaten
1 tbsp chopped dill
2 tbsp chopped parsley
salt and pepper, to taste
breadcrumbs (optional)

Empanadas

1. For the pastry, crumble the yeast and mix with the milk and sugar. Put the flour into a bowl and make a well in the centre. Add the egg yolks, butter and yeast mixture and knead to a smooth, heavy dough. Add a little more flour or milk if necessary (the dough should be neither sticky nor crumbly). Shape into a ball, put into the bowl, cover with cling film and chill overnight.

2. For the filling, heat the oil and gently cook the onion and garlic until soft. Add the red pepper and jalapeños and cook for 5 minutes.

3. Add the meat and cook, breaking it up with a fork to brown right through. Season with salt and pepper.

4. Mix together the egg, crème fraîche, tomato purée and chopped parsley and stir into the meat mixture. Add a few breadcrumbs if the mixture is too soft. Season with salt and pepper and add chilli powder to taste.

5. Roll out the dough thinly on a floured surface and cut out 12–15cm circles with a round cutter.

6. Put a little of the filling in the middle of each circle, fold the pastry over the filling and press the edges together firmly (twist the edges with the prongs of a fork or roll the edges over to make a decorative twist).

7. Preheat the oven to 400°F (200°C). Grease a baking tray. Whisk the egg yolks with 1–2 tablespoons water and brush over the dough. Place on the baking tray and bake for 15–20 minutes, until golden brown. Serve hot or cold.

Preparation time: 25 min
  plus overnight chilling
Cook time: 40 min
Serves 6–8

For the pastry:
10g yeast
4 tbsp warm milk
A pinch of sugar
300g plain flour
1 pinch salt
2 egg yolks
200g butter

For the filling:
1 tbsp oil
1 onion, finely chopped
1 garlic clove, finely chopped
1 red pepper, finely chopped
2–3 tbsp finely chopped jalapeños
400g minced steak
1 egg, whisked
4 tbsp crème fraîche
1–2 tbsp tomato purée
A bunch of parsley, chopped
chilli powder
1–2 tbsp breadcrumbs (optional)
2 egg yolks

Chimicurri sauce

1. Blend all the ingredients in a mini food blender.

2. Serve the sauce alongside the empanadas for dipping.

Preparation time: 40 min
Cooking time: 20 min
Serves 14–16

*a handful of basil, flat leaf parsley
   and oregano
60ml extra virgin olive oil
juice of 1 lemon*

Bruschetta with tomatoes, olives and anchovies

Preparation time: 15 min
Cooking time: 5 min
Serves 4–6

2 baguettes, cut diagonally into
  slices
2 garlic cloves, cut in half
500g cherry tomatoes, skinned
2 tbsp olive oil
1–2 small butterhead lettuce
2 tbsp black olives, pitted, roughly
  chopped
20 anchovy fillets

1. Preheat the oven to 400°F (200°C). Grease a baking tray.

2. Rub the baguette slices with the cut garlic cloves and toast in the oven for about 5 minutes until golden brown. Leave to cool.

3. Season the tomatoes with salt and pepper and drizzle olive oil over the top.

4. Place a few lettuce leaves on the baguette slices, followed by the tomatoes, olives and anchovy fillets.

Herb omelette roulade with salmon and vegetable filling

1. Heat 1 tablespoon butter in a frying pan and cook the spring onions, carrots and tomatoes for 2–3 minutes, stirring. Season with salt and pepper and remove from the heat.

2. Whisk the eggs, milk, salt and pepper to taste, and stir in the cheese and herbs.

3. Heat the remaining butter in a frying pan. Pour in half the egg mixture and cook over a medium heat for 5 minutes, until set. Place the cooked omelette in a low oven to keep warm. Make a second omelette in the same way.

4. Mix together the vegetables, salmon and crème fraîche.

5. Spread the two omelettes with the vegetable mixture, season with salt and pepper and roll up carefully. Cut into slices to serve and garnish with parsley.

Preparation time: 10 min
Cooking time: 15 min
Serves 4

2 tbsp butter
2 spring onions, finely chopped
2 carrots, grated
4 tomatoes, diced
8 eggs
8 tbsp milk
110g grated Gruyère
2 bunches mixed herbs, finely
  chopped
200g smoked salmon, thinly sliced
6 tbsp crème fraîche
salt and pepper, to taste
parsley, to serve

Parmesan wafers with Parma ham and figs

1. Preheat the oven to 350°F (180°C). Line a baking tray with non-stick baking paper.

2. Place a large round biscuit cutter (about 10cm diameter) on the baking tray and spread a thin, even layer of grated cheese inside it. Remove the biscuit cutter and repeat the process 7 more times, to make 8 Parmesan wafers.

3. Cook for about 5 minutes until the cheese melts and bubbles, and turns golden brown. Cool slightly on the baking tray, then remove from the tray and place on a wire rack to cool completely.

4. Top 4 Parmesan wafers with ham and fig wedges and cover each with a second wafer.

Preparation time: 10 min
Cooking time: 5 min
Serves 4

200g grated Parmesan
4 slices Parma ham
2 figs, cut into wedges

Chickpea balls

1. Put the chickpeas, breadcrumbs, lemon zest and juice, spices and salt in a blender with the egg. Blend to a smooth paste.

2. Form into balls with moist hands.

3. Heat the oil in a deep pan and fry the balls until crisp and golden. Place on wooden cocktail sticks.

4. For the dip, mix together all the ingredients and serve alongside the chickpea balls.

Preparation time: 15 min
Cooking time: 10 min
Serves 4

For the chickpea balls:
225g canned chickpeas, drained
100g brown breadcrumbs
½ lemon juice and grated zest
1 tsp chilli powder
½ tsp ground cumin
1 tsp salt
1 egg
oil for deep-frying

For the dip:
3 tbsp mayonnaise
2 tbsp chilli sauce
1 tbsp tomato ketchup

Croissant with chicken, spinach and cream cheese

1. Preheat the oven to 400°F (200°C). Grease a baking tray.

2. Heat the oil in a frying pan and cook the chicken gently for about 3 minutes on each side, or until nearly cooked through. Remove from the pan and set aside.

3. Wilt the washed spinach in a large pan, drain, squeeze out any excess moisture and chop well.

4. Roll the pastry on a floured board into a rectangle of about 40cm x 30cm. Cut the rectangle in half lengthways, then cut each half diagonally so you have 4 triangles.

5. Mix the cream cheese with the lemon juice and season with salt and pepper. Place a chicken breast at the wide end of each triangle, spread with a little cream cheese and top with chopped spinach. Tuck the edges of the pastry in and roll up to make a croissant. Seal the edges well with a little water, brush with the beaten egg and cook on the baking tray for 15–20 minutes, until the pastry is golden brown.

Preparation time: 15 min
Cooking time: 30 min
Serves 4

2 tbsp vegetable oil
4 chicken breasts, skinned
2 handfuls spinach, washed
450g all-butter puff pastry
200g cream cheese
½ lemon, juice
1 egg, whisked

Lamb meatballs with minted yoghurt sauce

1. Mix the lamb with the shallot, parsley, oregano, lemon juice, salt and pepper and cinnamon. Form into 12 small balls.

2. Heat 2 tablespoons oil in a frying pan and fry the meatballs on all sides until cooked through.

3. For the sauce, mix the yoghurt with the remaining oil then stir in the garlic and mint. Season to taste with salt and pepper.

4. Serve the meatballs with the minted yoghurt sauce and garnish with oregano.

Preparation time: 15 min
Cooking time: 10 min
Serves 4

For the meatballs:
300g minced lamb
1 shallot, diced
3 tbsp chopped parsley
1 tsp dried oregano, plus extra to
  serve
2 tsp lemon juice
A pinch of cinnamon
3 tbsp oil
salt and pepper, to taste

For the sauce:
300ml plain yoghurt
1 garlic clove, finely chopped
2 tbsp chopped mint

Carpaccio of beef with horseradish and Parmesan

Preparation time: 20 min
 plus 20 min chilling
Serves 4

450g beef tenderloin
1 tbsp creamed horseradish
1 lemon, juice
2 tbsp olive oil
salt and pepper, to taste
50g Parmesan, shaved
1 handful rocket

1. Wrap the beef in cling film and place in the freezer for 20 minutes.

2. Slice the beef with a very sharp knife as thinly as possible and lay the slices on a serving platter or 4 individual plates.

3. Dot the creamed horseradish over the beef, drizzle over the lemon juice and oil, and sprinkle with salt and pepper.

4. Scatter over the cheese and rocket and serve immediately.

Tuna in spring roll pastry with lime dip

1. Mix the wasabi paste with 1 tablespoon water. Season the tuna sticks with salt and pepper.

2. Brush the tuna sticks with the wasabi and roll in the chopped herbs.

3. Lay one fish stick on each sheet of spring roll pastry.

4. Whisk the egg yolk with the remaining water, brush the edges of the pastry and roll up.

5. Heat the oil in a deep pan and fry the rolls in batches for about 5 minutes until golden brown.

6. For the dip, mix the lime juice and soy sauce and serve with the tuna rolls.

Preparation time: 15 min
Cooking time: 10 min
Serves 8

1 tbsp wasabi paste
2 tbsp water
400g tuna fillet, cut into 8 sticks
salt and pepper, to taste
3 tbsp finely chopped coriander
  leaves
3 tbsp finely chopped parsley
8 sheets spring roll pastry
1 egg yolk, beaten
oil for deep-frying

For the dip:
75ml lime juice
75ml light soy sauce

Mushroom and cranberry ragout crostini

1. Heat 2 tablespoons of oil in a frying pan and fry the mushrooms and cranberries over a high heat for 3–4 minutes, stirring. Season to taste with salt and pepper.

2. Toast the baguette slices. Rub with the cut garlic.

3. Mix the mushroom mixture with the remaining olive oil and the Parmesan and spoon onto the baguette slices.

Preparaction time: 10 min
Cooking time: 10 min
Serves 4

4 tbsp olive oil
250g button mushrooms, sliced
70g cranberries
salt and pepper, to taste
8 baguette slices
2 garlic cloves, halved
2 tbsp coarsely grated Parmesan

Spinach and ricotta pasties

1. Put the flour into a mixing bowl with the salt and oil, and mix well. Add the lukewarm water and knead to a pliable dough. Cover and leave to rest at room temperature for about 30 minutes.

2. Preheat the oven to 350°F (180°C). Grease a baking sheet.

3. Put the spinach into a pan with a little salted water and cook over a high heat, stirring occasionally, until it wilts. Drain, rinse in cold water and drain thoroughly. Squeeze out the spinach and chop finely.

4. Mix together the spring onions, ricotta, spinach, lemon zest and egg and season to taste with salt, pepper and nutmeg.

5. Knead the dough on a lightly floured surface. Roll out thinly and cut into 10cm squares.

6. Put a little filling on each square and fold in half diagonally. Press the edges together with a fork.

7. Put the pasties on the baking sheet. Whisk the egg yolk with the milk, and brush over the pasties. Bake for about 25 minutes until lightly browned.

8. Garnish with mint.

Preparation time: 15 min
  plus 30 min resting
Cooking time: 30 min
Serves 4

For the pastry:
200g plain flour
1 tsp salt
1 tbsp oil
125ml lukewarm water
1 egg yolk, beaten, to glaze
1 tbsp milk, to glaze

For the filling:
500g spinach
½ bunch spring onions, chopped
250g ricotta
1 tsp grated lemon zest
1 egg
grated nutmeg

To garnish:
mint leaves

Deep-fried rice balls

Preparation time: 20 min
Cooking time: 40 min
Serves 4

500ml water
300g short-grain rice
½ tsp saffron threads
2 tbsp hot water
50g grated Parmesan
2 tbsp butter
2 eggs
150g mozzarella cheese, diced
2 tbsp flour
4–5 tbsp breadcrumbs
oil, for deep frying
bay leaves, to serve

1. Put the water and rice into a pan with a pinch of salt. Bring to a boil and cook over a very low heat, stirring frequently, until the water has been absorbed.

2. Dissolve the saffron in the hot water and stir into the rice with the Parmesan. Leave to cool slightly, then stir in the butter and 1 egg.

3. Whisk 1 egg in a deep plate and season lightly with salt and pepper.

4. Form the cooled rice into 10 balls about the size of a mandarin orange. Make a depression in the centre with your finger and fill with the diced cheese. Seal the opening.

5. Dust the rice balls with flour and roll first in egg and then in breadcrumbs.

6. Heat the oil in a deep pan and fry the rice balls, a few at a time, until golden. Drain on kitchen paper.

7. Place on a serving plate and garnish with bay leaves.

Vol-au-vent with turkey and mushroom filling

1. Heat 1 tablespoon butter in a frying pan and cook the shallots and mushrooms until soft. Remove from the pan.

2. Toss the turkey in the cornflour.

3. Heat 1 tablespoon butter in the pan and cook the turkey in batches, until cooked through.

4. Add the mushroom mixture to the pan, then add the crème fraîche, cream, vermouth and Worcestershire sauce and cook gently over a low heat for about 10 minutes, until the sauce is creamy. Season to taste with salt and pepper and stir in the parsley.

5. Spoon the filling into the vol-au-vent cases and garnish with the parsley leaves.

Preparation time: 15 min
Cooking time: 20 min
Serves 4

3 tbsp butter
2 shallots, chopped
250g button mushrooms, diced
300g turkey breast, diced
2 tbsp cornflour
75 ml crème fraîche
125 ml double cream
2 tbsp vermouth
1 tsp Worcestershire sauce
salt and pepper, to taste
6–8 ready made vol-au-vent cases
1 tbsp finely chopped parsley, plus
*   extra leaves to serve*

Pumpkin with cranberry relish

1. Mix the cranberries with the concentrated pear juice, orange juice and diced apple.

2. Heat 1 tablespoon oil in a frying pan and gently cook the onion until translucent. Add the cranberry mixture and cook gently for 3 minutes. Season to taste with salt and pepper and leave to cool.

3. Heat the remaining oil and cook the pumpkin until tender.

4. Pour in the stock, cover and cook gently for 10 minutes.

5. Serve with the cranberry relish and garnish with the herbs.

Preparation time: 15 min
Cooking time: 25 min
Serves 4

250g cranberries
4 tbsp concentrated pear juice
120ml orange juice
2 dessert apples, diced
2 tbsp oil
1 onion, diced
salt and pepper, to taste
500g pumpkin flesh, sliced
50ml stock
4 sprigs each thyme and basil,
  to serve

Making aioli (garlic mayonnaise)

Aioli is a classic and fragrant mayonnaise flavoured with garlic. It is most often served with seafood or shellfish, but it also makes a delicious dip for fresh chopped vegetables.

STEP 1 Put some mustard and a finely chopped clove of garlic into a large, clean mixing bowl. Separate the eggs, tipping the yolks into the ingredients.

STEP 2 Add vinegar to the egg yolks, and, using a hand whisk, beat lightly to combine the ingredients.

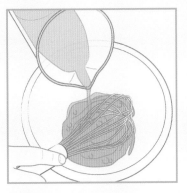

STEP 3 Begin to add the olive oil, pouring it into the egg mixture a little drizzle at a time and whisking after each addition.

STEP 4 Continue to whisk the mixture well until it begins to thicken and the emulsion stabilises.

STEP 5 When all the oil has been whisked in and the aioli is thick, stir in some lemon juice to taste.

Blini with crab and bean salad

1. Dissolve the yeast in the milk and leave to stand for 10 minutes until frothy.

2. Mix both flours in a mixing bowl and stir in the yeast mixture, with melted butter, egg yolks and salt. Cover and leave to rise in a warm place for about 50 minutes.

3. Whisk the egg whites until stiff and fold into the mixture.

4. Heat a little butter in a frying pan and place tablespoonfuls of the mixture in the pan. Flatten slightly and fry on both sides until golden brown. Remove from the pan and keep warm.

5. Blanch the beans in salted boiling water for 8 minutes. Rinse in cold water, then drain well.

6. Mix the crème fraîche with the tomato purée, ketchup, cayenne pepper and a little salt.

7. Stir in the crayfish or crab meat and beans.

8. Top each blini with 1–2 tablespoons of the mixture and garnish with basil.

Preparation time: 20 min
  plus 1 h standing
Cooking time: 20 min
Serves 20

For the blini:
20g fresh yeast
300ml lukewarm milk
150g buckwheat flour
150 plain flour
2 tbsp melted butter
2 eggs, separated
A pinch of salt
butter, for frying

For the topping:
250g green beans, sliced
300ml crème fraîche
1 tsp tomato purée
2 tbsp tomato ketchup
½ tsp cayenne pepper
500g crayfish or crab meat, flaked

To garnish:
basil

Avocado salsa on Lebanese flatbread

1. Peel the avocados, halve lengthways and remove the stones. Remove the flesh from the skin and dice finely.

2. Mix the avocados with the onion, lime juice and parsley. Season to taste with salt and pepper.

3. Serve the avocado salsa on warmed flatbread.

Preparation time: 15 min
Serves 4

2 ripe avocados
1 red onion, diced
1 lime, juice
½ bunch parsley, chopped
salt and pepper, to taste
1 packet Lebanese flatbread

Spring rolls with ricotta and sweet chilli sauce

1. For the sauce, bring the sugar and water to a boil and simmer until the mixture turns into a clear syrup.

2. Stir in the tomato paste, salt, vinegar and chilli and let cool.

3. For the filling: heat 2 tablespoons oil in a frying pan and fry the paneer cubes until golden brown.

4. Wilt the spinach in the remaining oil and continue frying until steamed dry.

5. Mix together the spinach, pepper, spring onions, garlic, chilli, paneer, lemon zest and ricotta and season with salt and pepper.

6. Divide the mixture between the sheets of pastry.

7. Fold in the ends of the pastry squares and roll up. Brush the edges with water and press firmly to close.

8. Deep fry the spring rolls in hot oil for around 5 minutes a few at a time until golden brown.

9. Serve with the chilli sauce.

Preparation time: 25 min
Cooking time: 25 min
Serves 4

*16 sheets frozen filo pastry, approx.
  300g in total, separated and
  thawed*

For the sauce:
40g sugar
4 tbsp water
1 tbsp tomato paste
1 tsp salt
1 tbsp rice vinegar
*1 red chilli pepper, very finely
  chopped*

For the filling:
6 tbsp vegetable oil
*200g paneer cheese, chopped into
  cubes*
100g spinach
1 red pepper, chopped
3 spring onions, chopped
2 garlic cloves, finely chopped
1 green chilli pepper, finely chopped
½ tsp lemon zest, finely grated
100g ricotta cheese
oil, for deep frying

Gazpacho

Preparation time: 20 min
 plus 1 h chilling
Serves 4

500g ripe tomatoes
½ cucumber, peeled and finely
 diced
1 red pepper, finely diced
2 Spanish onions, quartered
1 tbsp white wine vinegar
2 garlic cloves, crushed
1 tsp sugar
1 tsp sweet paprika
1 tbsp ground almonds
2 tbsp olive oil
salt and pepper, to taste

1. Put the tomatoes into a bowl and cover with boiling water. Stand for 1 minute, then remove the skins.

2. Set aside 1 tablespoon of the cucumber and 1 tablespoon of the pepper for garnishing.

3. Put all the ingredients into a blender and blend until smooth, adding enough cold water to make the required consistency.

4. Season with salt and pepper. You may also want to add more sugar.

5. Chill for at least 1 hour, then serve in glasses with the reserved diced cucumber and red pepper as a garnish.

Hot Camembert topped with nuts

1. Preheat the oven to 400°F (200°C). Line a baking sheet with non-stick baking paper.

2. Place the Camembert on the baking sheet.

3. Mix the nuts with the oil and spread on top of the cheeses. Bake for about 8–10 minutes until the cheese has melted. Serve immediately.

Preparation time: 10 min
Cooking time: 10 min
Serves 4

4 round Camembert cheeses
50g chopped walnuts
1 tbsp walnut oil

Spanish vegetable tortilla

1. Preheat the oven to 350°F (180°C). Grease a baking dish.

2. Heat the olive oil and gently cook the onion until soft. Add the red pepper and cook for 3 minutes.

3. Add the sliced potatoes, garlic, tomato, peas, parsley and thyme and cook for 3 minutes. Season with salt and place in the baking dish.

4. Whisk together the milk, eggs and spices and pour over the vegetable mixture.

5. Bake for about 25–35 minutes, until the eggs are set and lightly browned.

6. Garnish with olives and thyme.

Preparation time: 15 min
Cooking time: 45 min
Serves 4

3 tbsp olive oil
1 onion, finely chopped
1 red pepper, diced
300g cooked potatoes, thinly sliced
2 garlic cloves, crushed
1 tomato, diced
125g peas
2 tbsp chopped parsley
1 tsp thyme leaves, plus sprigs to
 serve
100ml milk
8 eggs
½ tsp curry powder
½ tsp paprika
grated nutmeg
black olives, to serve

Puff pastry squares with tomato and fresh basil

1. Preheat the oven to 425°F (220°C). Grease a baking sheet.

2. Lay the puff pastry sheets on top of one another and roll out thinly on a floured surface. Cut 6 rectangles of about 8 x 10cm. Cut out strips 1cm wide from the scraps of pastry.

3. Brush the edges of the rectangles with the egg yolk then stick the remaining pastry strips on the edges to form a rim. Place on the baking tray.

4. Spread the tomatoes and mozzarella over the pastry bases, sprinkle with balsamic vinegar and oil, and season with salt and pepper. Scatter with oregano and finely chopped basil.

5. Bake for about 15–20 minutes until golden. Serve immediately, garnished with basil leaves.

Preparation time: 15 min
Cooking time: 20 min
Serves 4–6

300g puff pastry sheets
1 egg yolk, beaten

For the topping:
700g ripe tomatoes, cut into wedges
300g mozzarella cheese, sliced
1 tbsp balsamic vinegar
2 tbsp olive oil
½ tsp dried oregano
2 tbsp chopped basil, plus extra
  to serve
salt and pepper, to taste

Marinated courgettes on wooden cocktail sticks

Preparation time: 15 min
  plus 1 h 20 min resting
Cooking time: 15 min
Serves 4–6

800g courgettes, thinly sliced
6 tbsp olive oil
3 garlic cloves, finely chopped
1 chilli, finely chopped
30ml white wine vinegar
basil leaves
salt and pepper, to taste

1. Spread the courgette slices on a plate. Sprinkle lightly with salt and leave to rest for 20 minutes, then pat dry.

2. Heat 2 tablespoons oil in a frying pan and put in enough courgette slices to cover the base of the pan. Fry for 1 minute on each side, then drain and set aside. Repeat the process with the remaining courgette slices, adding more oil for each batch.

3. Fry the garlic in the remaining oil until translucent. Add the chilli and briefly fry both together.

4. Add the vinegar, ½ teaspoon salt and a pinch of pepper, stir and pour over the courgettes. Cover and leave to marinate for 1 hour.

5. Thread on to wooden sticks with basil leaves.

Puff pastry rolls with mince and pepper filling

1. Preheat the oven to 425°F (220°C). Grease a baking sheet.

2. Heat the oil in a frying pan and cook the meat and vegetables for 4 minutes, stirring. Mix in the parsley, season to taste with salt and pepper and set aside to cool.

3. Lay the pastry sheets out in pairs (one on top of the other) on a lightly floured surface and roll out to rectangles of about 20 x 30cm.

4. Spread with the filling, leaving a margin of about 1.5cm around the edges. Fold the pastry in on the narrow sides and roll up from the long side.

5. Place on the baking sheet. Whisk the egg yolk with the milk and brush over the rolls.

6. Bake for about 25 minutes, until golden brown. Cool slightly and cut into 5cm pieces.

Preparation time: 15 min
Cooking time: 30 min
Serves 12–15

2 tbsp oil
200g minced meat
1 red pepper, diced
2 sticks celery, diced
½ bunch spring onions, chopped
2 tbsp parsley, chopped
salt and pepper, to taste
6 sheets puff pastry
1 egg yolk
2 tbsp milk

Spanish meatballs with sherry sauce

1. For the sauce, put the tomatoes into boiling water for a few seconds, then skin, halve, deseed and dice.

2. Heat the oil in a frying pan and cook the onion until soft. Add the tomatoes, cover and simmer for about 20 minutes, stirring frequently.

3. Add the sherry and season to taste with salt and pepper.

4. For the meatballs, mix the breadcrumbs with the sherry and leave to stand for 10 minutes.

5. Toast the pine nuts in a dry frying pan.

6. Add the meat, pine nuts, onion, garlic and olives to the breadcrumbs and season to taste with salt and pepper. Add the cumin and mix well to produce a shapeable mixture. Shape into small balls and roll in the flour.

7. Heat the olive oil in a frying pan with the bay leaves and fry the meatballs on all sides over a fairly high heat until cooked through.

8. Place the meatballs on plates and serve the sherry sauce separately.

Preparation time: 15 min
    plus 10 min standing
Cooking time: 25 min
Serves 4

For the sauce:
1kg ripe tomatoes
2 tbsp olive oil
1 onion, chopped
200ml sherry

For the meatballs:
50g fresh white breadcrumbs
6 tbsp sherry
4 tbsp pine nuts
500g minced meat
1 large onion, chopped
1 garlic clove, chopped
50g olives, pitted and chopped
A pinch of ground cumin
2 tbsp flour
2 bay leaves
6 tbsp olive oil

Grilling aubergines

The 'meaty' texture of aubergines makes these vegetables perfect for grilling, and an ideal ingredient for a vegetarian main-course dish. Salting isn't essential, but it does reduce the amount if oil needed to cook them.

STEP 2 Using a large, sharp knife, cut the aubergine lengthwise into five or six thick slices. There's no need to peel away the skin first.

STEP 3 Sprinkle a little salt evenly over the cut sides of the aubergine slices. Place in a colander and set aside for 30 minutes. Rinse and pat dry.

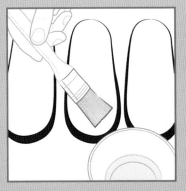

STEP 4 Place the aubergine slices on a chopping board or work surface and brush one side with olive oil using a pastry brush.

STEP 5 Heat a griddle until very hot, then add the slices in one layer and cook until lightly browned. Turn over, oil the other side and cook until browned.

Stuffed mushrooms with chorizo on cocktail sticks

1. Preheat the oven to 425°F (220°C). Grease a baking dish.

2. Cut 16 thin slices from the chorizo and finely dice the rest.

3. Finely chop the mushroom stalks.

4. Heat the oil in a frying pan and fry the mushroom stalks, onion and garlic for 5 minutes.

5. Add the parsley and the diced chorizo, then stir in the sherry and cook until it has evaporated.

6. Remove from the heat and mix with the breadcrumbs and cheese. Season with salt, pepper and paprika.

7. Spoon into the mushroom caps and place in the baking dish. Cook for about 10 minutes until the mushrooms are browned and the filling is hot.

8. Place each stuffed mushroom on a slice of chorizo, securing with a wooden cocktail stick.

Preparation time: 15 min
Cooking time: 20 min
Serves 4

450g piece chorizo
16 large button mushrooms
1 tbsp olive oil
1 onion, finely chopped
2 garlic cloves, finely chopped
2 tbsp finely chopped parsley
2 tbsp dry sherry
1 tbsp breadcrumbs
1 tbsp grated cheese
½ tsp mild paprika powder

Canapés with smoked salmon, cream cheese and capers

1. Toast the bread and cut out circles using a large cutter.

2. Mix the cheese with salt, pepper and lemon juice and put a spoonful on each slice of toast.

3. Arrange the salmon on the cheese. Mix the capers with the parsley and put a little on top of the salmon.

Preparation time: 10 min
Serves 4

12 slices wholemeal bread
150g cream cheese
1 tbsp lemon juice
12 slices smoked salmon
1 tbsp capers
1 tbsp chopped parsley

Asparagus salad with strawberries

1. Peel the lower third of each green asparagus stalk and cut off the ends. Peel the whole of each white asparagus stalk and cut off the ends.

2. Cook the white asparagus in boiling water with the sugar, butter and lemon juice for 5 minutes. Cook the green asparagus for 5 minutes. Drain, retaining the cooking liquid, rinse the asparagus in cold water and drain again.

3. Cut each asparagus spear into 3 and mix with the strawberries.

4. Mix together a little of the asparagus water with salt, pepper, vinegars and oil. Check the seasoning.

5. Toss the asparagus and strawberries in the dressing and divide between serving bowls.

Preparation time: 20 min
Cooking time: 5 min
Serves 4

500g green asparagus
500g white asparagus
1 tsp sugar
1 tbsp butter
juice of ½ lemon
400g strawberries, quartered
3 tbsp balsamic vinegar
3 tbsp strawberry vinegar
3 tbsp sunflower oil

Deep-fried sardines or whitebait

Preparation time: 10 min
Cooking time: 10 min
Serves 4

100g flour
a pinch of salt
a pinch of cayenne pepper
400g sardines or whitebait
100ml milk
oil, for deep frying
lemon wedges, to serve

1. Mix the flour with the salt and cayenne pepper.

2. Coat the fish in the flour, shake off any excess and dip briefly in the milk, then dip back into the flour. Shake off the excess flour.

3. Heat the oil until very hot and fry the fish in 2 or 3 batches, for 3–4 minutes until crisp. Drain on kitchen paper.

4. Serve immediately with lemon wedges.

Crostini alla crema di olive

1. Preheat the oven to 400°F (200°C). Grease a baking tray.

2. Rub the bread slices with the cut cloves of garlic and drizzle with 2 tablespoons olive oil. Put on the baking tray and cook for 5–8 minutes, until golden.

3. Put the olives, capers, pine nuts, tomato paste, vinegar and remaining olive oil into a blender and process to a paste. Season to taste with pepper.

4. Spread on the bread slices and garnish with sliced tomatoes and coriander leaves.

Preparation time: 10 min
Cooking time: 8 min
Serves 12

12 baguette slices
2 garlic cloves, halved
4 tbsp olive oil
125g black olives, pitted
1 tbsp capers
1 tbsp pine nuts, toasted
2 tbsp tomato paste
2 tsp balsamic vinegar
pepper, to taste
sliced tomatoes and coriander
*   leaves, to serve*

Tuna empanadas

1. Heat the olive oil and gently cook the onion until translucent. Add the tuna and pepper and fry for 2 minutes, stirring. Season with salt and chilli powder, then stir in the parsley and leave to cool.

2. Preheat the oven to 400°F (200°C). Line a baking tray with non-stick baking paper.

3. Cut the sheets of puff pastry in half to produce 20 rectangles.

4. Put 1 teaspoon of the filling on 1 half of each pastry rectangle, fold the other half over and press the edges together firmly. Press around the edges with a fork. Round off the corners with a sharp knife, making sure the edges stay pressed together. Cut small fish shapes out of the trimmings.

5. Place on the baking tray a little distance apart.

6. Whisk the egg yolk and milk together and brush over the pastry. Place the pastry fish on top, press lightly and bake for 25 minutes, until the pastry is crisp.

Preparation time: 20 min
Cooking time: 35 min
Serves 20

2 tbsp olive oil
1 onion, finely chopped
1 can tuna, drained
1 yellow pepper, diced
½ tsp chilli powder
½ bunch parsley, finely chopped
10 sheets ready-rolled puff pastry
1 egg yolk
2 tbsp milk

Mini-quiches with peas and ham

1. For the pastry, put the flour in a mixing bowl and stir in the salt. Rub in the butter until the mixture resembles breadcrumbs. Break the egg into the middle, knead it to a dough with your hands and form into a ball. Wrap in cling film and chill for about 30 minutes.

2. Preheat the oven to 400°F (200°C). Grease 4 mini quiche tins.

3. Roll out the pastry on a floured surface and line the tins. Prick the base with a fork and bake for about 10 minutes until golden.

4. Reduce the oven temperature to 350°F (180°C).

5. For the filling, mix together the cooked and raw ham, onion, peas, chives and garlic.

6. Whisk the eggs and stir in the cheese and cream. Season to taste with salt and pepper.

7. Spoon the pea and ham mixture into the pastry cases, pour the cheese and cream mixture over and bake for about 35 minutes until the filling is set. Serve with a green salad.

Preparation time: 20 min
plus 30 min chilling
Cooking time: 45 min
Serves 4

For the pastry:
250g plain flour
A pinch of salt
125g butter
1 egg

For the filling:
50g cooked ham, diced
50g mild raw ham, diced
1 onion, finely chopped
150g peas
1 bunch chives, snipped
3 garlic cloves, finely chopped
4 eggs
200g grated Gruyère cheese
200ml double cream

Feta cheese wrapped in courgette with rosemary

Preparation time: 10 min
Cooking time: 10 min
Serves 20 rolls

3–4 medium-sized courgettes
salt and pepper, to taste
2 tbsp oil
250g feta
10 rosemary sprigs, cut in half
extra virgin olive oil

1. Cut the courgettes into 20 wafer-thin slices lengthwise (use a mandoline, if available).

2. Heat the oil in a frying pan and fry the courgette slices on both sides, a few at a time, until lightly browned. Season with salt and pepper. Drain on kitchen paper and leave to cool.

3. Cut the feta into 20 small, even pieces and wrap each in a slice of courgette. Secure with half a rosemary sprig.

4. Place the courgette rolls on serving plates in a pool of olive oil.

Green beans with Parma ham

1. Blanch the beans in salted boiling water for 6–8 minutes. Drain well.

2. For the sauce, clarify the butter by melting it and skimming off the foam.

3. Put the egg yolks and wine into a heatproof bowl and beat over a pan of simmering (not boiling) water until foamy.

4. Add the butter, in drops at first, then in a thin stream, beating constantly to a creamy, homogenous sauce. Do not let the mixture boil as the egg yolks will curdle. Season with salt and pepper and add lemon juice to taste.

5. Drain the beans. Divide into 8 bundles, carefully wrap a slice of Parma ham around each bundle and tie with a chive.

6. Serve on warmed plates, sprinkle with a little sauce and serve the rest of the sauce separately.

Preparation time: 15 min
Cooking time: 15 min
Serves 4

800g green beans
8 slices Parma ham
8 thick chives

For the sauce:
250g butter
2 egg yolks
4 tbsp dry white wine
salt and pepper, to taste
2 tbsp lemon juice

Deep-fried corn fritters

1. Put half the sweetcorn into a food processor with the minced pork, garlic, sugar, eggs and cornflour. Process until smooth.

2. Tip into a bowl and stir in the remaining sweetcorn, adding a little more cornflour if necessary. Season to taste with fish sauce and cayenne pepper.

3. Heat the oil and fry spoonfuls of the mixture for 2–3 minutes, turning occasionally, until golden brown. Drain on kitchen paper and serve speared on toothpicks.

Preparation time: 15 min
Cooking time: 10 min
Serves 4

400g canned sweetcorn, drained
150g minced pork
2 garlic cloves
1 tbsp sugar
2 eggs
1 tbsp cornflour
fish sauce
cayenne pepper
oil, for deep-frying

Savoury carrot cake with cress

1. Preheat the oven to 350°F (180°C). Grease a 1 kg loaf tin.

2. Whisk the eggs with the oil and salt. Sift in the flour with the baking powder, then stir in the pine nuts, parsley and Parmesan. Add the carrots and season with salt and pepper.

3. Spoon into the loaf tin and bake for 50–60 minutes, until cooked through. Cool in the tin for 5 minutes, then place on a wire rack to cool completely.

4. For the filling, mix together all the ingredients until smooth.

5. Split the cake horizontally and spread the bottom half with the filling, using all but 4 tablespoons. Replace the top half of the cake and neaten the edges.

6. Pipe or spoon the remaining filling in blobs on top of the cake and garnish with baby carrots and cress.

Preparation time: 25 min
Cooking time: 1 h
Serves 10–12 slices

For the cake:
4 eggs
100ml olive oil
1 tsp salt
300g plain flour
3 tsp baking powder
50g pine nuts
1 tbsp chopped parsley
50g grated Parmesan
200g finely grated carrots

For the filling:
200g cream cheese
100ml double cream
1 tsp horseradish sauce

To garnish:
cooked baby carrots
cress

Duck terrine with green pepper and onion chutney

1. Put the duck in a bowl with the orange and lemon juices and marinate for 2 hours. Heat oven to 400°F (200°C). Line an ovenproof terrine dish with ovenproof foil, allowing the foil to hang over the edge. Heat 2 tablespoons oil in a frying pan and cook the shallots until soft. Remove the duck from the marinade. Set aside the duck breast fillets.

2. Mince the remaining duck meat with the pork and bacon. Stir in the shallots, pistachios, peppercorns and marinade. Season with salt, pepper and lemon zest. Heat 1 tablespoon oil in the pan and brown the duck breast fillets for 3–4 minutes. Set aside to cool. Wrap each fillet in a slice of ham. Heat the remaining oil in the pan and brown the duck liver on all sides. Season with salt and a little cayenne pepper. Chop the liver into small pieces. Mix the liver pieces with the minced meats and put half into the terrine dish.

3. Lay the wrapped duck breast fillets on top, lengthwise. Press lightly and put the rest of the minced meats on top. Smooth the top and cover with the overhanging foil. Tap the dish to settle the contents. Cover and place in a roasting tin half-filled with hot water. Bake for 45 minutes, until cooked through. Add more hot water to the tin if necessary. Cool and chill overnight.

4. For the chutney: heat the butter and gently cook the onions for 5–7 minutes until translucent. Add the vinegars and syrup, stir in the icing sugar and bring to a boil. Simmer for 30–35 minutes. Season with salt and pepper and leave to cool.

Preparation time: 30 min
plus 2 h marinating and overnight chilling
Cooking time: 1 h 20 min
Serves 4

For the terrine:
2 duck breast fillets, skinned
2 duck legs, skinned and boned
juice and grated zest of 1 lemon
juice of 1 orange
4 tbsp oil
3 shallots, chopped
125g pork fillet
250g unsmoked bacon
50g pistachios, chopped very finely
1 tsp green peppercorns, crushed
2 slices cooked ham
250g duck liver
cayenne pepper

For the chutney:
80g butter
500g onions, cut into rings
100ml sherry vinegar
150ml red wine vinegar
40ml Grenadine syrup
75g icing sugar

Yellow tomatoes stuffed with couscous

1. Heat the stock and pour over the couscous. Leave to stand for about 5 minutes, then fluff with a fork.

2. Cut off the tops of the yellow tomatoes and hollow out. Discard the seeds and dice the remaining flesh.

3. Put the red tomato into boiling water for a few seconds, then skin, quarter, deseed and dice.

4. Mix the couscous with the red tomato, diced yellow tomato and garlic. Add the cucumber, chopped basil, lemon juice and oil, and mix well.

5. Season to taste with salt and cayenne pepper and fill the hollowed-out tomatoes with the mixture. Replace the tops and garnish with basil.

Preparation time: 15 min
Cooking time: 10 min
Serves 4

200ml vegetable stock
200g couscous
4 yellow tomatoes
1 red tomato
1 garlic clove, finely chopped
½ cucumber, peeled and diced
1 bunch basil, finely chopped,
*   plus extra to serve*
½ lemon, juice
4 tbsp olive oil
salt
cayenne pepper

Baked stuffed aubergines topped with ham

Preparation time: 15 min
Cooking time: 35 min
Serves 4

oil, for deep frying
4 aubergines, halved
2 tbsp olive oil
1 onion, finely chopped
2 red peppers, finely chopped
2 large ripe tomatoes, finely
  chopped
1 tbsp tomato paste
3 tbsp lemon juice
a pinch of sugar
4 slices Parma ham, cut in half
spring onions, to serve

1. Heat the oil in a deep pan and fry the aubergines until soft inside and browned on the outside. Drain on kitchen paper.

2. Preheat the oven to 350°F (180°C). Grease a baking dish.

3. Heat the olive oil in a frying pan and cook the onion and peppers until soft. Add the tomatoes, tomato paste, sugar and salt and pepper to taste and cook slowly for 7–8 minutes.

4. Place the aubergines in the baking dish and drizzle with lemon juice. Spoon in the filling and bake for 20–25 minutes until piping hot.

5. Place the aubergines on a serving plate and place the ham on top. Garnish with whole and finely chopped spring onions.

Patatas bravas

1. Preheat the oven to 350°F (180°C). Grease a baking tray.

2. Put the potatoes on the baking tray. Sprinkle with olive oil and sea salt and cook for about 20 minutes, turning several times, until golden brown.

3. Drop the tomatoes into boiling water for a few seconds, then skin, quarter, deseed and dice.

4. Heat 2 tablespoons oil in a frying pan and gently cook the onion and garlic until translucent. Stir in the tomato purée and tomatoes. Simmer for 6–8 minutes.

5. Add sugar, salt and Tabasco to taste.

6. Put the potatoes into bowls, spoon the tomato sauce over and serve sprinkled with oregano.

Preparation time: 15 min
Cooking time: 30 min
Serves 4

600g potatoes, peeled and diced
olive oil
sea salt
6 tomatoes
1 onion, diced
1 garlic clove, finely chopped
1 tbsp tomato purée
sugar
salt
Tabasco sauce
1 tbsp chopped oregano

Figs stuffed with blue cheese and walnuts

1. Cut a cross in the top of each fig (do not cut right through) and open it up slightly.

2. Mix the blue cheese into the cream cheese. Season to taste with salt and pepper.

3. Fill the figs with the blue cheese mixture. Place a walnut half on top of each.

Preparation time: 15 min
Serves 4

8 large ripe figs
100g blue cheese, diced
200g cream cheese
salt and pepper, to taste
8 walnut halves

Momos – steamed dumplings with a meat filling

1. For the dough, knead together the flour, salt, oil and lukewarm water. Cover and allow to rest for 1 hour.

2. For the filling, mix the meat with the garlic, onion and spring onion, and season with salt and garam masala. Add the ginger.

3. Make 12–16 small balls out of the dough and roll out on a floured board into thin circles.

4. Place 1 tablespoon of the filling in the middle of each one. Fold the edges inside and press together,

5. Place the momos in a greased colander and steam for about 15 minutes over a pot of boiling water. Serve with chilli sauce.

Preparation time: 25 min
  plus 1 h resting
Cooking time: 15 min
Serves 4

For the dough:
500g plain flour
1 tsp salt
1 tbsp vegetable oil
175ml lukewarm water

For the filling:
350g beef, e.g. fillet or loin, finely
  chopped
1 garlic clove, finely chopped
1 onion, finely chopped
1 spring onion, finely chopped
½ tsp garam masala
2cm fresh root ginger, grated

Chilli polenta cakes

Preparation time: 30 min
plus 5 h chilling
Cooking time: 20 min
Serves 4

6 tbsp olive oil
2 shallots, finely chopped
1 litre vegetable stock
2 green chillies, finely diced
1 green pepper, diced
1 tsp chopped rosemary leaves
250g polenta
6 tbsp grated Parmesan
1 tbsp chopped parsley
2 tbsp butter

To garnish:
spring onion rings
onion strips
black peppercorns, crushed
chives

1. Heat 2 tablespoons olive oil in a pan and cook the shallots until translucent.

2. Add the stock and bring to a boil. Add the chillies, peppers and rosemary, and gradually trickle in the polenta, stirring constantly. Simmer gently for 1–1 ½ minutes until the polenta starts to swell. Cover, set aside and leave to stand for 10 minutes.

3. Reheat the polenta and mix with 4 tablespoons grated Parmesan, the chopped parsley, 2 tablespoon olive oil, butter, salt and pepper to taste and stir until creamy.

4. Turn the polenta into the tray, spread evenly and brush the surface with the remaining olive oil. Leave to cool at room temperature for 1 hour and then chill in the refrigerator for 4 to 5 hours.

5. Preheat the oven to 350°F (180°C). Brush a deep baking sheet with a little olive oil. Cut out small cakes (6–7cm in diameter) from the polenta with a round cutter. Place on the baking sheet and sprinkle with the remaining Parmesan. Bake for 5–8 minutes.

6. Garnish with spring onion rings, onion strips, peppercorns and chives.

Marinated tuna in lemongrass vinaigrette

1. Put the tuna in a shallow bowl.

2. Mix together the vinegar, lemon juice, oil and salt, and pour over the fish. Scatter with lemon zest, lemongrass, shallot and mint.

3. Cover and leave to stand for 1 hour before serving.

Preparation time: 10 min
  plus 1 h standing
Serves 4

500g very fresh tuna fillet,
  thinly sliced
4 tbsp white wine vinegar
juice and grated zest of 1 lemon
150ml olive oil
¼ tsp salt
2 stalks lemongrass, sliced
1 shallot, finely chopped
1 tbsp finely chopped mint leaves

Deep fried squid rings with aioli dip

1. For the aioli, beat the egg yolks until creamy then add the garlic, pepper, mustard and salt.

2. Beat in the oil, a drop at a time, until the mixture starts to thicken, then add the rest of the oil in a thin stream, beating constantly, until you have a creamy mayonnaise. Add the lemon juice, check the seasoning and set aside.

3. For the squid, mix the flour with the white wine and egg yolks to make a smooth batter, stir in the salt and leave to stand for about 10 minutes.

4. Whisk the egg whites until stiff and fold into the batter.

5. Heat the oil in a deep pan until just smoking. Dust the squid rings with the flour, dip into the batter and fry in batches until golden brown. Drain on kitchen paper and serve with the aioli alongside.

Preparation time: 30 min
  plus 10 min standing
Cooking time: 20 min
Serves 4

For the aioli:
2 egg yolks
6 garlic cloves, crushed
1 tsp black peppercorns, crushed
½ tsp mustard powder
1 tsp salt
400ml olive oil
juice of 1 lemon

For the squid:
200g flour, plus extra for dusting
250ml white wine
2 eggs, separated
½ tsp salt
500ml sunflower oil
600g squid tubes, cleaned and sliced
  into rings

Making crostini and croutes

Toasted chunks of bread make delicious light lunches, snacks or starters when topped with tomatoes, cheese or other ingredients, or for mopping up tapas. They are easy to make and are perfect for using up day-old bread.

STEP 1 Cut a baguette or ciabatta into slices using a bread knife, cutting slightly at an angle to get larger, oval pieces.

STEP 2 Cut a garlic clove in half and rub the cut side over one side of a piece of bread. Repeat with the remaining slices of bread.

STEP 3 Drizzle some olive oil over the same side of the bread and place onto a very hot griddle pan. Cook until chargrilled lines appear.

STEP 4 Remove the toasts from the griddle and top them with the ingredient of your choice. Serve warm.

CROUTES are prepared in the same way as the bread for crostini, but cut the bread slices much thinner.

Grilled calamari with lime dressing

1. Mix the vinegar, lime juice, cream and oil to make the dressing. Stir in the parsley, season with salt and pepper and set aside.

2. Heat a griddle pan or grill to medium heat. Wash the calamari rings and pat dry. Brush with the remaining oil and cook for about 4 minutes, turning once.

3. Serve the calamari on beds of rocket with the dressing drizzled over and lime wedges to serve.

Preparation time: 15 min
Cooking time: 5 min
Serves 4

1 tbsp white wine vinegar
2 tbsp lime juice
3 tbsp single cream
3 tbsp olive oil
1 tbsp parsley, finely chopped
675g calamari rings
1 bunch rocket
lime wedges, to serve

Shrimps fried in coconut batter with lemon mayonnaise

1. For the mayonnaise, beat the egg yolks until creamy, then add the pepper, mustard and salt.

2. Mix together the olive and sunflower oils and beat into the egg yolks, a drop at a time, until the mixture starts to thicken, then add the rest of the oil in a thin stream, beating constantly, until you have a creamy mayonnaise. Add the lemon juice, check the seasoning and set aside.

3. Peel the prawns, leaving the tails attached and remove the black veins. Rinse well and pat dry with kitchen paper.

4. Heat the oil in a deep pan until just smoking. Sprinkle the coconut with the paprika, mix well and put onto a saucer.

5. Dip the prawns into the beaten egg white, then coat with the coconut mixture. Deep-fry the prawns in the oil for about 3 minutes or until golden brown. Drain on kitchen paper and serve with the lemon mayonnaise.

Preparation time: 30 min
Cooking time: 5 min
Serves 4

For the lemon mayonnaise:
2 egg yolks
1 tsp black peppercorns, crushed
½ tsp mustard powder
1 tsp salt
200ml olive oil
200ml sunflower oil
juice of 1 lemon

For the prawns:
600g raw tiger prawns
500ml sunflower oil
100g grated coconut
½ tsp paprika
1 egg white, lightly beaten

Triple-decker pumpernickel squares

1. Put the basil into a blender and purée finely. Mix with 200g cream cheese and season to taste with salt and pepper. Chill.

2. Mix 200g cream cheese with the diced pepper, chilli powder, ajvar and ketchup and season to taste.

3. Mix the remaining cream cheese with the horseradish.

4. Spread 4 slices of pumpernickel with each of the spreads and place one on top of the other. Put the last 4 slices on top of each stack and chill. When well chilled, cut into cubes and arrange on a platter.

Preparation time: 30 min
Serves 4

1 bunch basil
600g low-fat cream cheese
salt and pepper, to taste
1 red pepper, finely diced
a good pinch of chilli powder
1 tbsp ajvar
1 tbsp ketchup
2 tbsp grated horseradish
16 slices pumpernickel bread

Smoked salmon terrine

Preparation time: 30 min
  plus 12 h chilling
Serves 4–6

5 gelatine leaves
250g quark
150g cream cheese
2 tbsp creamed horseradish
salt and pepper, to taste
1 tbsp lemon juice
1 tsp grated lemon zest
150ml double cream
400g smoked salmon, thinly sliced
1 tbsp chopped dill
1 stick celery, chopped

1. Line a loaf tin with cling film.

2. Soak the gelatine in a small bowl of cold water.

3. Mix the quark, cream cheese and horseradish and season to taste with salt, pepper, lemon juice and lemon zest.

4. Put the gelatine, dripping wet, into a small pan and dissolve over a very low heat.

5. Mix the gelatine with 2 tablespoons of the cream cheese mixture, then stir the gelatine mixture into the remaining mixture.

6. Whisk the cream until thick and fold into the cheese mixture.

7. Chop one-third of the smoked salmon and mix into the cheese mixture with the dill and chopped celery.

8. Line the base and sides of the loaf tin with salmon slices, letting the salmon overhang the edges. Fill with the cheese mixture and smooth the top. Fold the overhanging salmon slices over so that the cheese filling is completely enclosed. Cover and chill overnight.

Grilled red peppers with garlic

1. Heat the grill. Put the peppers under the grill, turning frequently, until the skins are charred all over.

2. Place the peppers in a large bowl, cover with cling film and let cool for 15 minutes.

3. Remove and discard the skins, stalks and seeds from the peppers.

4. Blend the olive oil with the lemon juice, season with salt and pepper and mix well with the peppers.

5. Arrange on a serving plate and scatter with the garlic and parsley.

Preparation time: 20 min
Cooking time: 10 min
Serves 4

6 long red peppers
125ml olive oil
juice of ½ lemon
salt and pepper, to taste
6 garlic cloves, roughly chopped
10g parsley, roughly chopped

Pumpkin strudel

1. Preheat the oven to 375°F (190°C). Line a baking dish with non-stick baking paper.

2. For the pastry, sift the flour and salt into a mixing bowl. Stir in the vinegar and lukewarm water and work until the dough does not stick to the hands.

3. Roll out on a floured surface, as thinly as possible, without tearing. Place a tablecloth on a table and put the rolled out dough on it. Pull gently with the hands, to get the dough as thin as tissue paper.

4. For the filling, sprinkle the pumpkin with a little salt and leave to stand for 20 minutes. Squeeze out the excess moisture and stir in the cheese, cream, butter and eggs.

5. Spread the filling over the dough. Take the tablecloth in both hands, and roll the strudel, over and over, holding the cloth high; the strudel will almost roll itself. Holding the edge of the cloth, roll the strudel into the baking dish.

6. For the topping, mix the egg and soured cream and pour over the strudel. Bake for 40–60 minutes until golden.

Preparation time: 1 h
Cooking time: 1 h
Serves 4

For the pastry:
400g flour
1 tsp salt
1 tsp white wine vinegar
200–300ml lukewarm water

For the filling:
500g pumpkin, grated
500g cottage cheese
200ml soured cream
50g butter, melted
2 eggs

For the topping:
1 egg
200ml soured cream

Carrot cakes with dried apricots

1. Peel the carrots and steam for about 20 minutes, until soft. Mash roughly and leave to steam dry.

2. Heat 2 tablespoons oil in a pan and gently cook the shallots and garlic until translucent.

3. Stir in the coriander, harissa, parsley and apricots. Remove from the heat and add the carrots, almonds, grated bread, egg, lemon juice and zest, and honey. Season to taste with salt and pepper.

4. Shape the mixture into about 20 small cakes.

5. Heat the oil in a frying pan and fry the carrot cakes in batches for 2–3 minutes on each side, until golden brown. Drain on kitchen paper.

6. Serve warm or cold, garnished with parsley and lemon wedges.

Preparation time: 20 min
Cooking time: 30 min
Serves 4

600g carrots
5 tbsp oil
2 shallots, finely chopped
2 garlic cloves, finely chopped
1 tsp ground coriander
1 tsp harissa
½ bunch parsley, chopped
80g dried apricots, chopped
100g almonds, toasted and chopped
5 slices stale white bread, grated
1 egg, whisked
½ lemon, grated zest and juice
1 tbsp honey
salt and pepper, to taste
parsley leaves and lemon wedges,
*   to serve*

Tomato carpaccio

Preparation time: 10 min
  plus 10 min standing
Serves 4

8 tomatoes, thinly sliced
150g yellow cherry tomatoes,
  quartered
½ bunch rocket
3 tbsp olive oil
2 tbsp white wine vinegar
salt and pepper, to taste
1 tsp dried oregano

1. Arrange the sliced tomatoes on a serving plate.

2. Scatter the cherry tomatoes over the sliced tomatoes. Add a few rocket leaves to the plate.

3. Sprinkle with oil and vinegar and season to taste with salt and pepper. Sprinkle with oregano and leave to stand for about 10 minutes before serving. Serve with toasted white bread.

Chicken and pumpkin patties with parsley

1. Coarsely grate the pumpkin.

2. Heat 1 tablespoon oil in a pan and gently fry the shallots until translucent.

3. Add 3–4 teaspoons masala, cook for 2 minutes, then remove from the heat and leave to cool.

4. Mix the pumpkin, breadcrumbs, shallots, parsley, chicken, eggs, 2 tablespoons flour and season to taste with salt and pepper.

5. Make 16–20 patties, using the remaining flour to lightly coat each one. Heat the remaining oil in a skillet and fry the patties for 4 minutes each side. Serve with mango wedges and garnish with coriander.

Preparation time: 20 min
Cooking time: 20 min
Serves 4

400g pumpkin, peeled and deseeded
4 tbsp olive oil
6 shallots, finely chopped
3 tsp garam masala
150g wholemeal breadcrumbs
25g parsley, chopped
450g minced chicken
2 eggs
3 –4 tbsp flour
salt and pepper, to taste
mango wedges
coriander leaves, to garnish

Deep-fried sweet potato wedges

1. Peel the sweet potatoes and cut into wedges.

2. Drizzle with the olive oil, sprinkle with the thyme and chilli powder and season with plenty of salt and pepper. Massage the flavourings into each slice.

3. Heat the oil and cook the wedges for 5–8 minutes, until tender. Drain on kitchen paper and serve immediately.

Preparation time: 10 min
Cooking time: 10 min
Serves 4

2 large sweet potatoes
4 tbsp olive oil
2 tbsp chopped thyme
1–2 tsp chilli powder
salt and pepper, to taste
oil, for deep frying

Spring vegetable strudel

1. For the pastry, mix all the pastry ingredients in a mixing bowl and knead to a smooth dough. Shape into a ball, put on a plate, brush with oil, cover and leave to rest for about 30 minutes.

2. For the filling, heat the butter and gently cook the leek and onion until translucent.

3. Blanch the cabbage, mangetout and carrots in salted boiling water for 3 minutes, then rinse in cold water and drain well.

4. Mix the crème fraîche with the egg yolks and parsley. Stir in the vegetables and season to taste with salt, pepper and nutmeg.

5. Preheat the oven to 400°F (200°C). Grease a baking tray. Roll the pastry out to a rectangle on a floured tea towel, then stretch over with the backs of your hands until wafer thin. Spread the pastry out on the tea towel and cut off any thick edges.

6. Sprinkle with breadcrumbs and lay the slices of ham on the pastry. Spread the filling on top of the ham.

7. Fold in the left and right edges of the pastry, then loosely roll up the strudel using the tea towel. Place join-side down on the baking tray and brush with melted butter.

8. Bake for 30–40 minutes until golden and crisp. Place on a serving plate and cut into slices to serve.

Preparation time: 20 min
plus 30 min resting
Cooking time: 1 h
Serves 4

For the strudel pastry:
200g plain flour
½ tsp salt
1 egg, beaten
2 tbsp oil
4 tbsp lukewarm water
1 tbsp oil, for brushing

For the filling:
2 tbsp melted butter
1 leek, sliced
1 onion, diced
400g white cabbage, shredded
300g mangetout
3 carrots, diced
100ml crème fraîche
2 egg yolks
2 tbsp chopped parsley
salt and pepper, to taste
grated nutmeg
breadcrumbs
150g ham, sliced
1 tbsp melted butter

Olive cake cubes

1. Sift the flour into a bowl with the yeast, salt and sugar.

2. Add the water and oil and mix to form a dough. Turn onto a floured board and knead for 5 minutes. Return to the bowl, cover and leave in a warm place to rise for 30 minutes.

3. Preheat the oven to 425°F (220°C). Grease a roasting tin.

4. Turn the dough onto a floured board and knead for 10 minutes. Stretch the dough across the board, sprinkle over the olives and ham and knead for 2 more minutes.

5. Spread the dough into the tin about 20cm x 25cm, brush with a little oil and bake for 25–30 minutes until risen and golden brown.

6. Turn out the bread, slice off the crusts and cut into bite-sized squares.

Preparation time: 40 min
  plus 30 min for rising
Cooking time: 30 min
Serves 4

225g strong bread flour
7g easy blend yeast
1 tsp salt
2 tsp sugar
150ml water, hand hot
2 tbsp olive oil
100g olives stuffed with pimento,
  drained and chopped
100g cooked ham, chopped

Potato pancakes with cucumber salsa

1. Drain the potatoes and mix with the egg yolks, sugar, salt and flour.

2. Dissolve the yeast in the warm milk and leave to stand for about 15 minutes until frothy.

3. Add the yeast mixture to the potato mixture and mix well to produce a thick batter. Add a little more milk if the batter is too thick. Leave to stand until the batter has clearly increased in volume.

4. Whisk the egg whites until stiff and fold into the batter.

5. Heat the oil in a frying pan and put spoonfuls of the batter into the pan to make small pancakes. Fry on both sides until golden brown. Keep warm in the oven.

6. For the salsa, mix together the cucumber, peppers, chillies and lemon juice and season to taste with salt and pepper.

7. Put a little soured cream on each pancake, add a little salsa and serve garnished with parsley.

Preparation time: 20 min
 plus 1 h standing
Cooking time: 20 min
Serves 4–6

*1.25kg floury potatoes, peeled and
 grated*
4 eggs, separated
1 tsp sugar
1 tsp salt
375g plain flour
42g fresh yeast
4 tbsp warm milk
4 tbsp oil
parsley, to serve

For the salsa:
1 cucumber, diced
1 red pepper, finely diced
1–2 red chillies, finely diced
2 –3 tbsp lemon juice
a pinch of salt
white pepper
200g soured cream

Courgette cakes

Preparation time: 20 min
Cooking time: 10 min
Serves 4

5 tbsp olive oil
1 onion, finely chopped
4 courgettes, grated
4 tbsp plain flour
salt and pepper, to taste
mint leaves, to serve

1. Heat 2 tablespoons oil in a pan and gently fry the onion until soft.

2. Mix the onion with the grated courgettes and the flour, season with salt and pepper and shape into small patties.

3. Heat the remaining oil in a frying pan and fry the patties for 3 minutes on each side or until golden brown.

4. Drain on kitchen paper and serve immediately, garnished with mint.

Crepes on cocktail sticks with fruit and syrup

1. Put the flour, salt, sugar, eggs and egg yolk into a bowl and beat to a smooth batter.

2. Add the milk and mineral water, stir in the melted butter and leave to stand for 1 hour.

3. Heat the butter in a frying pan. With a small ladle, pour some crepe mixture into the pan and swirl the pan to ensure the mixture is evenly spread over the base. Fry until light brown, turn over with a palette knife and fry the other side. Make 8 crepes in this way and keep warm in the oven.

4. Halve the crepes, fold again and spear on cocktail sticks. Decorate with the berries and pieces of fruit and arrange on plates. Serve with maple syrup.

Preparation time: 10 min
plus 1 h standing
Cooking time: 15 min
Serves 4

110g plain flour
a pinch of salt
3 tbsp sugar
2 eggs
1 egg yolk
100ml milk
100ml mineral water
2 tbsp melted butter
25g butter
raspberries, blueberries, pineapple
cubes and maple syrup, to garnish

Sausage rolls

1. Preheat the oven to 400°F (200°C). Grease a baking tray.

2. Mix together the Worcestershire sauce, Tabasco sauce, thyme and sausage meat and season well with salt and pepper.

3. Roll out the puff pastry into a large rectangle, then cut into 2 long rectangles.

4. Place a layer of sausage meat mixture down the middle of each pastry rectangle, then brush each with beaten egg on one edge.

5. Fold the other side of the pastry over onto the egg-washed edge. Press down to seal and trim any excess. Cut each pastry roll into 8–10 small sausage rolls.

6. Place the sausage rolls on the baking tray and bake for 15–20 minutes, until crisp and golden and the sausage meat is cooked through. Serve with wholegrain mustard.

Preparation time: 20 min
Cooking time: 20 min
Serves 16–20

1 tbsp Worcestershire sauce
1 tbsp Tabasco sauce
1 tbsp dried thyme
450g sausage meat
salt and pepper, to taste
450g ready-rolled puff pastry
1 egg, beaten

Grilled mussels

1. Scrub the mussels thoroughly, remove the beards and scrape off any deposits.

2. Cook the mussels in a large pan of boiling water for 5 minutes. Drain and discard any unopened mussels.

3. Discard the top shells, leaving the mussels in the lower shells.

4. Heat the grill.

5. Mix together the butter, olive oil, tomatoes, salt and pepper and garlic.

6. Spoon into the shells on top of the mussels and sprinkle with the cheese.

7. Grill for 2–3 minutes until sizzling. Serve in the shells and garnish with basil.

Preparation time: 15 min
Cooking time: 10 min
Serves 4

1kg mussels
1 tbsp butter, melted
2 tbsp extra virgin olive oil
4–5 tomatoes, finely chopped
2 garlic cloves, finely chopped
salt and pepper, to taste
6 tbsp grated Parmesan
basil leaves, to serve

Canapes with organic chorizo and stuffed olives

Preparation time: 15 min
Cook time: 10 min
Serves 12

½ tsp olive oil
½ tsp chilli powder
¼ tsp paprika
12 whole almonds
12 large green olives, pitted
12 baguette slices
1 tbsp extra virgin olive oil
12 slices organic chorizo

1. Preheat the oven to 375°F (190°C). Grease a baking tray.

2. Stir together the oil, chilli powder and paprika. Add the almonds, tossing to coat.

3. Place on a baking tray and bake for 8–10 minutes until dark and roasted. Leave to cool.

4. Stuff each olive with an almond and place on a cocktail stick.

5. Drizzle the extra virgin olive oil over the bread slices and place a slice of chorizo on top. Put a stuffed olive on top of each slice.

Hummus

1. Drain the chickpeas and put into a pan. Cover with water and bring to a boil. Cover and boil for 1–1½ hours until tender. Drain well and leave to cool.

2. Put in a food processor with the garlic, lemon juice and zest, tahini and salt. Blend together and pour in the olive oil as the motor is running.

3. If necessary add some cold water, still with the motor running, until you get the consistency you want. Add more salt if needed.

4. Spoon into a serving dish and garnish with olives, lemon wedges and parsley leaves. Serve with flatbread.

Preparation time: 10 min
   plus overnight soaking
Cooking time: 1 h 30 min
Serves 4

125g dried chickpeas, soaked in
*   water overnight*
2 garlic cloves
juice and grated zest of 1 lemon
2 tbsp tahini
salt, to taste
120ml olive oil

To garnish:
black olives
lemon wedges
parsley

Rice paper rolls with vegetable filling and soy sauce

1. Soften the rice paper between moist tea towels.

2. Mix the vinegar, oil, salt and pepper to taste.

3. Put 1–2 lettuce leaves on each sheet of rice paper, top with a few strips of carrot and pepper and some beansprouts. Sprinkle with the dressing.

4. Turn in the ends and roll up carefully. Cut each roll in half diagonally. Serve with soy sauce separately.

Preparation time: 20 min
Serves 4

4 sheets rice paper
1 tbsp white wine vinegar
3 tbsp olive oil
salt and pepper, to taste
1 small lettuce
2 carrots, cut into thin strips
1 red pepper, cut into strips
1 handful beansprouts

Preparing peppers

All peppers – red, yellow or green – can have a rather thick skin which not everyone finds easy to digest, and which when cooked can spoil the texture of the flesh. It's easy enough to remove.

STEP 1 Slice the pepper in half lengthwise, cutting through the green stem, using a sharp kitchen knife.

STEP 2 Working on each half at a time and using a sharp paring knife, cut away the white membrane and remove, taking with it the seeds and stem.

STEP 3 Grill the pepper halves on the skin side or toast over an open flame (using tongs) until blackened. Place in a plastic bag and seal tightly.

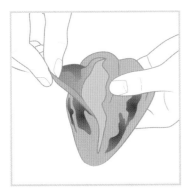

STEP 4 Once the peppers are cool enough to handle, remove them from the bag and, using fingers, begin to peel away the skin from the flesh.

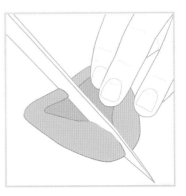

STEP 5 Wipe over the skinned peppers to remove any stray bits of skin, then place on a chopping board, insides up, and slice into chunks or strips.

Pork stir-fry served in lettuce cups

1. Mix together the fish sauce, 1 tablespoon oil and half the chilli strips. Add the meat and stir well. Cover and leave to marinate for 30 minutes.

2. Cook the noodles according to the packet instructions. Drain well and set aside.

3. Heat 2 tablespoons oil in a wok or frying pan, add the meat (reserve the marinade) and stir-fry for 1 minute until browned. Remove and set aside.

4. Add the remaining chilli strips, garlic, leek and mushrooms and stir-fry for 1–2 minutes.

5. Stir in the meat, marinade and sugar and cook for 3 minutes. Stir in the noodles.

6. Spoon into lettuce leaves just before serving.

Preparation time: 10 min
  plus 30 min marinating
Cooking time: 10 min
Serves 4

2 tbsp fish sauce
3 tbsp vegetable oil
1 green chilli, cut into strips
400g pork fillet, thinly sliced
350g thin Asian egg noodles
oil, for frying
2 garlic cloves, finely chopped
1 leek, cut into thin strips
150g shiitake mushrooms, sliced
1 tsp sugar
1 small lettuce

Pan-roasted oysters on toast

1. To open each oyster, hold the oyster in one hand in a kitchen cloth, rounded side down and insert the point of an oyster knife next to the hinge. Twist to open and slide the knife along inside the top shell to release the muscle attaching the oyster to the shell. Remove the top shell then loosen the oyster from the bottom shell.

2. Remove all the oysters from their shells and drain on kitchen paper.

3. Heat the olive oil in a frying pan and cook the oysters for about 1–2 minutes, so that they stew rather than fry. Sprinkle with lemon juice and season with pepper.

4. Remove from the pan. Place an oyster on each baguette slice, scatter with diced tomatoes and garnish each with lemon zest.

Preparation time: 15 min
Cooking time: 2 min
Serves 4

12 oysters
2 tbsp olive oil
juice of ½ lemon
12 slices baguette, toasted
4 tbsp diced tomatoes
lemon zest, to serve
pepper, to taste

Lettuce and ham rolls

1. Mix the diced tomatoes with the cheese, 1 tablespoon pine nuts and 1 teaspoon cress.

2. For the dressing: mix together all the ingredients and stir half of the dressing into the tomatoes and cheese.

3. Lay out the iceberg lettuce leaves and cover each with a slice of ham. Divide the lollo rosso and radicchio between them.

4. Add a little of the tomato and sheep's cheese mixture to each and roll up. Secure with cocktail sticks.

5. Put the lettuce and ham rolls on a serving plate, sprinkle with the remaining dressing and serve scattered with the remaining cress and the remaining pine nuts.

Preparation time: 30 min
Serves 4

Ingredients:
2 tomatoes, finely diced
50 g Feta cheese, diced
2 tbsp pine nuts, toasted
2 tsp cress
8 iceberg lettuce leaves
8 slices cooked ham
4 lollo rosso leaves, torn in half
4 radicchio leaves, shredded

For the dressing:
1 tbsp lemon juice
1 tbsp olive oil
salt and pepper, to taste
1 pinch sugar
1 good pinch medium-hot mustard

Pupusas with dipping sauce

Preparation time: 25 min
plus 10 min resting
Cooking time: 25 min
Serves 4

For the dough:
300g masa (a type of cornmeal)
200ml warm water
200g cottage cheese
oil, for deep-frying

For the Salsa Roja (dipping sauce):
3 tbsp olive oil
3 tbsp chopped onions
1 garlic clove, chopped
1 serrano or jalapeño chilli, finely
chopped
400g tomatoes, skinned, seeded
and chopped
2 tsp dried oregano

To garnish:
lettuce leaves

1. For the dough, put the masa and water into a mixing bowl, mix together and knead well. Add more water, a tablespoonful at a time if necessary, to produce a moist, but firm dough. (It should not crack at the edges when you press down on it.) Cover and leave to rest for 5–10 minutes.

2. Roll the dough into a log and cut into 8 equal portions.

3. Roll each portion into a ball. Press an indentation into each ball with your thumb and put about 1 tablespoon of cottage cheese into the indentation. Fold the dough over to enclose the filling and carefully press the filled balls with the palms of your hands to make round discs.

4. Heat the oil in a deep pan and fry the pupusas until golden brown. Drain on kitchen paper.

5. For the sauce, heat the oil in a pan and gently cook the onion, garlic and chilli for 2–3 minutes, until the onion is translucent.

6. Add the tomatoes and oregano, and simmer for 10 minutes. Remove from the heat and cool slightly. Purée in a blender until smooth, adding a little water if necessary. Season to taste with salt and pepper.

7. Serve the pupusas on plates with a small dish of sauce and a garnish of lettuce.

Small pasties with curried mushroom filling

1. Mix together the flour, salt, water, egg and butter in a mixing bowl to form a dough. Knead well, wrap in cling film and leave to rest for about 1 hour.

2. For the filling, heat the butter in a frying pan and cook the onion until translucent. Add the mushrooms and pepper and sprinkle with curry powder, salt and pepper, and fry over a low heat for 6 minutes. Remove from the heat, cool slightly, and stir in the parsley.

3. Roll out the pastry thinly on a surface dusted with flour. Cut out 8cm squares. Brush the edges with a little egg yolk.

4. Spread the filling on the pastry squares, fold over once and press the edges together firmly.

5. Heat the oil in a deep pan and fry the filled parcels in batches until lightly browned. Drain on kitchen paper and keep warm in the oven.

6. Serve with lime wedges.

Preparation time: 15 min
  plus 1 h resting
Cooking time: 15 min
Serves 4

For the dough:
350g plain flour
½ tsp salt
100ml water
1 egg, beaten
2 tbsp melted butter

For the filling:
2 tbsp butter
1 onion, diced
200g small button mushrooms,
  sliced
1 red pepper, diced
1 tsp curry powder
salt and pepper, to taste
2 tbsp chopped parsley
1 egg yolk, beaten
oil, for deep frying

To serve:
lime wedges

Grilled tomatoes with herbs and toasted garlic bread

1. Preheat the oven to 325°F (170°C). Grease a baking dish.

2. Put the tomatoes in the baking dish, cut side up, and drizzle with the olive oil and balsamic vinegar.

3. Season to taste with salt and pepper and sprinkle with the herbs.

4. Cook for 40–50 minutes until soft. Serve with toasted garlic bread.

Preparation time: 15 min
Cooking time: 50 min
Serves 4

1kg plum tomatoes, halved
2 tbsp olive oil
2 tbsp balsamic vinegar
2 tbsp chopped herbs, (oregano, thyme, rosemary)
salt and pepper, to taste
garlic bread, to serve

Bean and cheese quesadillas

1. Preheat the oven to 400°F (200°C). Line a baking tray with non-stick baking paper.

2. Heat the oil in a frying pan and cook the garlic, chillies and bacon until browned.

3. Stir in the tomato concentrate and water, followed by the beans and simmer for 2–3 minutes. Season with cayenne pepper and salt.

4. Spread the bean mixture on the tortillas, cover with grated cheese and fold in half.

5. Place on the baking tray and bake for about 10 minutes until golden brown.

Preparation time: 10 min
Cooking time: 20 min
Serves 4

1 tbsp oil
1 garlic clove, finely chopped
2 mild green chillies, cut into rings
200g bacon, diced
1 tbsp tomato concentrate
4 tbsp water
400g canned red kidney beans,
  drained
cayenne pepper, to taste
salt, to taste
4 tortillas
100g grated Cheddar cheese

Avocado and tomato salad with prawns and basil

Preparation time: 10 min
Cooking time: 2 min
Serves 4

300g prawns
2 avocados, peeled and diced
juice of 1 lemon
1 tsp grated ginger
1 garlic clove, finely chopped
4 tomatoes, diced
2 tbsp sunflower oil
2 tbsp grapeseed oil
a pinch of sugar
cayenne pepper
2 tbsp chopped basil

1. Devein the prawns, then wash and pat dry.

2. Mix the avocado with the lemon juice, ginger, garlic and tomatoes.

3. Heat the sunflower oil in a frying pan and cook the prawns for 1–2 minutes.

4. Place the salad in serving bowls and put the prawns on top.

5. Mix together the grapeseed oil, sugar, a pinch of salt and cayenne pepper. Drizzle over the salads and serve immediately, sprinkled with chopped basil.

Sigara Böregi

1. Mix the feta with the herbs.

2. Cut each sheet of rice paper diagonally into 4 triangles.

3. Place on a surface with the triangle point facing upwards, parallel to the bottom side.

4. Spread 1 tablespoon of the filling on each triangle and roll up towards the tip. Brush the top with water to stick. Repeat with the remaining rice paper sheets and filling.

5. Heat the oil in a deep pan and fry the rolls for 2–3 minutes until golden brown. Drain on kitchen paper and serve immediately.

Preparation time: 15 min
Cooking time: 4 min
Serves 4

400g feta cheese, crumbled
2 tbsp chopped parsley
2 tbsp chopped dill
1 tbsp chopped mint
4 sheets rice paper, about 25 x 25cm
oil, for deep frying

Marinated sardines

1. Split the fish open and remove the backbones.

2. Put the fennel, onion, peppercorns, salt, water, wine and lemon slices into a pan. Bring to the boil and simmer for 5 minutes.

3. Add the sardines and cook for 5–10 minutes, until the fish is cooked. Set aside to cool.

4. Drain off the liquid and place the sardines in a shallow dish with the olive oil, fennel, parsley and garlic. Discard the lemon slices. Cover and leave to stand for about 4 hours before serving.

Preparation time: 15 min
plus 4 h marinating
Cooking time: 15 min
Serves 4

500g fresh sardines
1 small fennel bulb, finely diced
1 onion, finely chopped
1 tsp peppercorns
¼ tsp salt
250ml water
250ml dry white wine
1 lemon, sliced
½ bunch parsley, finely chopped
1 garlic clove, crushed
olive oil, to cover

Making a Spanish tortilla

Tortilla makes a delicious main course, hot from the pan, or can be cut up and eatencold at a picnic or as part of a tapas menu. Slice it into wedges or little chunks served on cocktail sticks, along with a glass of chilled sherry.

STEP 1 Heat some olive oil in a large frying pan with a heatproof handle and add the onion and potato. Cover with a lid and gently cook until soft.

STEP 2 In a large mixing bowl, lightly beat together the eggs with a little seasoning. Add the cooked onions and potatoes and mix gently.

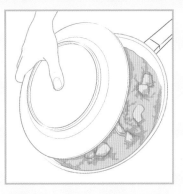

STEP 3 Return the mixture to the pan and place it in a medium oven. Cook for 15–20 minutes or until the eggs are just set. Place a plate over the pan.

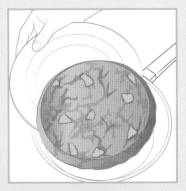

STEP 4 Using the plate, turn the pan over to gently tip out the tortilla. You may need to loosen the edges first.

STEP 5 Cut into wedges and eat at once, or set aside to cool, then chill before eating it cold.

Artichoke with mustard vinaigrette

1. Stand the artichokes side by side in a wide pan, half fill with water and add the lemon juice. Cover and cook over a medium heat for 25–30 minutes, until the leaves pull away easily.

2. For the vinaigrette, mix the vinegar, mustard and garlic. Whisk in the oil and season well.

3. Drain the artichokes well and serve on plates with a small dish of vinaigrette.

Preparation time: 10 min
Cooking time: 30 min
Serves 4

4 artichokes
juice of ½ lemon

For the vinaigrette:
2 tbsp white wine vinegar
2 tsp Dijon mustard
1 garlic clove, finely chopped
6 tbsp olive oil
salt and pepper, to taste

Beans and grilled tomatoes crostini

1. Preheat the oven to 400°F (200°C).

2. Mix the lemon juice, oil and crushed garlic and season with salt and pepper.

3. Mix the haricot beans, onions, lemon zest and parsley and stir in the dressing.

4. Put the tomatoes into the oven and roast for 15 minutes.

5. Toast the bread and rub with the garlic halves.

6. Pile spoonfuls of the vegetable mixture on each slice and top with rocket and the tomatoes. Serve immediately.

Preparation time: 15 min
Cooking time: 15 min
Serves 4

juice and zest of 1 lemon
4 tbsp olive oil
1 garlic clove, crushed, plus 1 cut in half
salt and pepper, to taste
200g canned haricot beans, drained and rinsed
1 red onion, finely chopped
2 tbsp parsley, finely chopped
4 bunches tomatoes, on the vine
8 slices rustic Italian white bread, or ciabatta
2 handfuls rocket

Chicken satay with peanut sauce

1. Mix the chicken with the remaining ingredients and marinate the meat for at least 2 hours.

2. Heat the grill.

3. Remove from the marinade, drain and thread onto 8–12 wooden skewers. Grill for about 10 minutes, brushing with the marinade from time to time.

4. For the sauce, toast the peanuts in a dry frying pan, then leave to cool and crush finely in a mortar.

5. Put the coconut milk, peanut butter and curry powder into a pan and bring to a boil.

6. Stir in the crushed peanuts, lemon juice and zest and add sugar to taste. Stir in the cream to produce a creamy sauce.

7. Serve the chicken skewers drizzled with peanut sauce.

Preparation time: 20 min
  plus 2 h marinating
Cooking time: 10 min
Serves 4–6

4 chicken fillets, diced
2 garlic cloves, crushed
1 small red chilli, finely chopped
1 shallot, finely chopped
¼ tsp each ground cumin and
  coriander
2 tbsp light soy sauce
4 tbsp coconut milk
2 tbsp oil

For the peanut sauce:
150g unsalted shelled peanuts
200ml coconut milk
2 tbsp peanut butter
1 tsp curry powder
juice and grated zest of 1 lemon
a pinch of sugar
3 tbsp double cream

Feta in herb marinade

Preparation time: 5 min
  plus overnight marinating
Serves 4

500g feta cheese, thickly sliced
1 red chilli, sliced
2 garlic cloves, sliced
50g black olives, pitted
1 sprig rosemary
5 sage leaves
2 sprigs thyme
1 stalk mint
200ml olive oil
peppercorns, lightly crushed

1. Place the feta in a shallow dish. Sprinkle with chilli, garlic, olives, herbs, salt, peppercorns and olive oil.

2. Cover and marinate overnight in the refrigerator.

Vietnamese spring rolls with asparagus and prawns

1. Spread the sheets of rice paper out separately between 2 damp tea towels.

2. Cook the asparagus in salted boiling water for 10 minutes, until cooked but still retaining a little bite. Drain well.

3. Heat 1 tablespoon sesame oil and briefly fry the prawns. Season with salt.

4. Mix together the remaining sesame oil, rice vinegar, chilli and fish sauce to make a dressing.

5. Place the sheets of rice paper together in twos, one on top of the other, and lay 1 lettuce leaf on each pair. Flatten slightly.

6. Put one prawn, some cucumber sticks, chives and asparagus in the middle of each, with the top of the filling level with one edge. Sprinkle with a little dressing.

7. Fold 1 side over the filling and then roll up firmly. Stick the edges with a little water.

Preparation time: 15 min
Cooking time: 10 min
Serves 4

16 sheets rice paper
150g green asparagus
3 tbsp sesame oil
8 prawns
1 tbsp rice vinegar
1 red chilli, finely chopped
1 tsp fish sauce
8 lettuce leaves
1 cucumber, cut into sticks
½ bunch chives, sliced

Prawn Pil Pil

1. Using a flameproof dish, heat the butter and oil until foaming. Add in the garlic and chilli. Cook until starting to turn golden.

2. Now add in the prawns and continue cooking until the prawns have turned pink, add in the paprika and continue cooking for a further 30 seconds before removing from the heat.

3. Sprinkle with the flat leaf parsley and serve with plenty of bread for dipping.

Preparation time: 5 min
Cooking time: 5 min
Serves 1 tapas portion

20g butter
2 tbsp olive oil
3 garlic cloves, finely chopped
1 small red chilli, finely chopped
10 peeled raw tiger prawns
1 tsp paprika
1 tbsp flat leaf parsley, finely chopped

Pimento padron

1. In a large frying pan or wok, heat the oil to smoking hot before adding in the peppers. Cook until blistered all over.

2. Sprinkle with plenty of Maldon salt and a splash of sherry vinegar. Serve immediately.

Preparation time: less than 5 min
Cooking time: 6 min
Serves 1 sharing portion

1 tbsp Spanish olive oil
300g pimento padrons
Maldon salt
a splash of sherry vinegar

Grilled prawns with ramanesco sauce

Preparation time: 20 min
Cooking time: 10 min
Serves 2

*8 peeled king prawns, head and
    tail on*
4 lemon wedges
4 bay leaves
2 bamboo or metal skewers

For the sauce
4 roasted red peppers
*3 ripe tomatoes roasted in the
    oven for 15 mins, skin removed*
15 toasted blanched almonds
10 toasted blanched hazelnuts
*4 garlic cloves, roasted and
    peeled*
2 tbsp stale bread
1 dried chilli
1 tbsp sherry vinegar
1 tsp smoked paprika
handful of flat leaf parsley
5 tbsp extra virgin olive oil

1. Place all the ingredients for the sauce in a food processor and blend until smooth.

2. Thread the prawns, lemon wedges and bay leaves onto skewer and place under a hot grill until pink.

3. Pour some of the sauce on to a plate and top with the grilled prawns.

Revuelto with asparagus and wild mushrooms

1. Cook the asparagus spears in a pan of boiled water for 3 minutes before removing and chopping.

2. Place the Serrano ham under a grill for 1–2 minutes until crispy, remove and reserve for later.

3. Heat a little olive oil in a pan, when the pan is hot, add in the mushrooms and cook for 2 minutes. Add in the garlic and cook for 1 minute.

4. Add the paprika to the beaten eggs along with some salt and pepper and mix. Add the egg to the pan and leave for 10 seconds before using a spatula to move the egg back and forth mixing the egg with the mushrooms. Add in the chopped asparagus while the eggs are still a bit runny and stir through.

5. Remove from the pan. Dust with a little paprika and top with the crispy Serrano.

Preparation time: 5 min
Cooking time: 5 min
Serves 1 tapas serving

6 fine asparagus spears
2 slices Serrano ham
olive oil
30g wild mushrooms
1 garlic clove, crushed
¼ tsp paprika, plus extra to dust
4 eggs, beaten
salt and pepper, to taste

Salmorejo soup

1. Blitz the tomatoes and garlic in a food processor before passing them through a sieve, pressing the solids to remove any juices. Discard any seeds.

2. Break the bread into walnut-sized chunks and place in a large bowl. Mix the olive oil and salt into the tomatoes and then pour this over the bread.

3. Squeeze the bread and tomato mixture together using your hands until combined. Leave to stand for 2 minutes.

4. Add to a blender along with the vinegar and enough chilled water to create a creamy smooth consistency.

5. Serve chilled, sprinkled with a little of the chopped egg, Serrano, parsley and green peppers.

Preparation time: 20 min
Serves 4

10 skinned ripe tomatoes
2 garlic cloves
80g stale white bread
4 tbsp extra virgin olive oil
2 tbsp red wine vinegar
2 hard-boiled eggs, finely chopped
2 slices of Serrano ham, finely chopped
1 tsp finely chopped parsley
1 tbsp green pepper, finely chopped

Index

Notes

Notes

Notes

Notes

Favourite recipes

Favourite recipes

Favourite recipes

Favourite recipes

Favourite recipes

Favourite recipes

Favourite recipes